Cats Believe in Santa

Tales of Finding a Forever Home

Jennifer B. Foulk & Robert F. Biser

J. B. Foulk Publishing

Cats Believe in Santa
Tales of Finding a Forever Home
All Rights Reserved.
Copyright © 2012 Jennifer B Foulk & Robert F Biser
v3.0

J. B. Foulk Publishing

PB ISBN: 978-0-578-09684-1

HB ISBN: 978-0-578-09723-7

PRINTED IN THE UNITED STATES OF AMERICA

For the Cats.
And for Dad,
because he Believes.
-JBF

To all the volunteers throughout the country who give of themselves to care for animals in need. For all the organizations dedicated to providing shelter and hope for lost, abandoned, injured, and newborn animals. May this book be a small token of thanks to them. We also hope to inspire others to donate whatever they can to help meet the continuing needs of cats and other animals throughout the year. More importantly, what they will give back to you is priceless.
-RFB

Contents

Introduction

In the cold blue light of late afternoon, giant snowflakes are falling silently. The cardinals and finches bustle about at the feeders, gobbling their precious day's supply of black oil sunflower seeds. Nearby, several chickadees clamor for a turn, while a few slate gray juncos take advantage of seeds that have already spilled to the ground. Everybody's feathers are fluffed out in attempts to keep warm in such frigid temperatures.

Out in the pasture, the horses paw the freshly fallen snow for late year grasses as they head down the hill to the barn for their second meal of the day. Their breath clouds the air as they stamp and snort and shake their heads in anticipation. In the distance, a lone male red fox methodically picks his way across the field, casually eyeing the horses as their ears perk up in interest. He heads for the brook in search of what is sure to be another paltry bachelor dinner. This year's kits are once again on their own in another part of the vast woods. He plods through the cold weather days, searching for meager sustenance and taking to his den early in the evenings, with little else to occupy his time. In a small clearing at the edge of the forest,

a doe cautiously makes her way, her fawn close behind. His small white tail wags back and forth intermittently as he explores below the surface of the snow with his nose. They, too, are searching for a bite to eat before returning to the warm shelter of their woodland nest. It is lovely to watch all of this through the large bay windows of the great room, looking out over the rolling pastures that comprise our backyard. From the comfort of a high-backed arm chair, my gaze turns to the crackling fire that has warmed my feet and filled the house with the delightful scent of hickory and pine. The Christmas tree looms majestically, sparkling with tiny white lights and ornaments, both aged heirlooms and newer treasures. Cinnamon, nutmeg, and vanilla are wafting in on dreamy waves of sweet goodness from the kitchen where Mom is baking. It is mid-December at Pine Brook Farm, and the Christmas season is well underway. Feelings of peace and contentment fill my heart as I gaze at the furry felines sleeping soundly in their various spots around the room, including my lap, where Quincy is purring happily. Together we look up at the sign hanging from the balcony that overlooks the room, emblazoned with the simple yet profound words, *"We Believe in Santa."* An identical sign graces the rafters in the barn, high above the horse stalls. What is perhaps more remarkable is that these yuletide beacons remain in place all year long. This is not out of neglect or procrastination in taking down holiday decorations, but rather because Christmas is a season of joyous sentiments that we, as a family, seek to remember and share the whole year through. I know in my heart that cats too, believe in the spirit of Santa Claus, just as we have since childhood. Our excitement over Christmas morning surprises has evolved to a simple appreciation for our loved ones. As our faithful and devoted friends, cats have always known the importance of this. They seek and find the goodness in us, returning so much more. When we remember the gifts our

feline friends share with us all year long, we pass that kindness along to others, one person at a time.

The stories presented here are about the cats of a horse farm in northern Maryland, where my parents have resided for nearly two decades. These tales highlight the ways our cats have touched our daily lives. The telling photographs were taken by

my father who, over the years, has never passed up an opportunity to capture that special moment or scene on film. Their home has become a beacon of friendship and comfort for all cats, along with the horses, birds, foxes, deer, and many other wild creatures that have claimed Pine Brook Farm as their sanctuary.

This is a book about the Spirit of Christmas and how this spirit is conveyed to us by our loving cats throughout the year. Read in December or June, may you be reminded of how much cats bring us companionship, laughter, and so many wonderful, warm memories. Those of you who have ever shared the joys of owning a cat will

surely appreciate this. And for those readers who've never had this experience, it is our sincere hope that these pages might inspire you to consider providing a much-needed, loving home for a cat without one.

Wishing you the very best, from our home to yours.

Abbey

Our family was never supposed to have cats. From birth until I reached high school, we were pretty much a two-pooch household. We didn't know anything about cats, and had mistakenly assumed that they were all very independent animals with little personality.

I grew up on a registered wildlife sanctuary, home to numerous bird species. Our backyard also housed an ornamental pond, complete with blooming water lilies, chirping frogs, and chubby goldfish. Between the dogs, birds, and fish it seemed clear that our house was just not the place for a cat. All that changed in December of 1990.

Dad had seen a small brown tabby cat playing in the sandbox near our tree house. He decided to trap her so she could be taken to our local humane society. A few days went by without success before the cat was caught following a cold, rainy night. She was clearly not happy as she growled and hissed in protest of her new accommodations. Dad brought the cage into our warm garage, gave her food, water, and a soft towel to lay on, and instructed my sister and I to "leave her be."

Of course the date was December 23rd, a Sunday,

and the humane society was closed until after Christmas. On the eve of the 24th, feeling terribly sorry for her, I stealthily made my way out to the garage under the auspices of ensuring that she had enough food.

I proceeded to talk to her softly in an effort to calm her down. The next thing I knew, Dad had come out to check on me after my lengthy absence and there she was, sitting with me and purring contentedly as I gently stroked her fur.

After witnessing this change in her disposition, someone mentioned that surely the garage was too damp, and we should really bring her inside. Within a few hours, she was sitting with us in the living room, enjoying the Christmas tree and a warm fire.

On Christmas Day, no one mentioned the words "humane society," for she had already rooted herself in our hearts. At some vague point during our peaceful celebration of Christmas that year, my parents decided that we would keep her.

And so Abbey the Tabby became the very first feline member in a long line of cats to grace our household, and she fit in just fine. She remained indoors, so there was no trouble for our feathered or finned friends. After a few squabbles, she eventually became quite attached to our dogs, often curling up beside them as they all drifted off to sleep together. Her unpleasant experience in the trap, however, was not forgotten. One afternoon my father was lying on the floor of the sunroom talking to her and telling her what a good cat she was, when she promptly walked over, stared him in the eye for a moment, and swatted his head as if to say, "And that's for leaving me in the cage overnight."

Like all of our cats, Abbey ended up with various nicknames over the years. My sister dubbed her "Moo" for reasons that remain unclear. As she aged, she began to put on weight, and would often conduct the preening of her underside while sitting up but somewhat hunched over. This earned her the title of "Buddha." And one of her most favorite places to sit was in the exact center of our kitchen table, usually on a freshly laundered tablecloth, with her paws neatly tucked under. She would look at us as if this was the most natural place for her to be while we referred to her as a "rump roast."

Abbey exhibited multiple personalities. One such example involved what came to be known as her "evening crazies," or the "Moo Express." She'd get that itch as all cats do from time to time, and start racing around the house, fur flying, back twitching. This usually happened at dinner time, and as she'd go sailing with her back end desperately trying to gain traction on the smooth kitchen floor, Mom would announce "…and it's the 7:18 Moo Express, right on time."

The Christmas that Abbey arrived was my last at home before college, so from then on, Mom kept me informed of her antics via much anticipated letters regularly delivered to my dormitory mailbox. One of my favorite excerpts was from a note dated November 7, 1991:

"Abbey is getting goofy in her advancing age. She also has a "thing" for my snake plant. I caught her right in the act. The other day, she was sitting on the chair when suddenly she reached over and took a crunchy bite out of one of the leaves. I yelled at her, "What do you think this is, the salad bar at Perkins?!" Poor plant will never be the same. Furthermore, Abbey has evil malice in her heart for my little pewter piggy thimble. It's sitting on the end table, next to the couch. I have some books there and the piggy-and-piglet thimble is on top of the books. Every time she gets "possessed," she quietly sashays along the back of the couch, slinks down onto the end table, stares at the little pewter porkers, then either sends them flying with one swipe or just gently taps them until they eventually end upon the floor."

Abbey would utter an ascending musical chirp when you touched her back gently and she wasn't expecting it. It sounded like she was asking, "Hmm?" I can recall many a phone call home when Mom would pause, say "Wait a minute," then put the phone near Moo and poke her so I could laugh at that sound from 800 miles away. Talk about reaching out and touching someone. It helped alleviate some of my homesickness until I could get back to the family for the holidays.

And so the adventure began with the rather chance arrival of Abbey the Tabby, a true gift at Christmas, and the very first to teach us about cats.

Sidney

Around the farm these days, Sidney is the most senior feline resident - and he must certainly enjoy our telling and re-telling of his youthful adventures. Sid came to us as a bedraggled orphan kitten of six weeks, peering out at my mother from behind some Black-eyed Susans as she was enjoying one of her summer evening walks. He wormed his way into our hearts and through the years has been largely known for his unwavering sense of mischief.

By far the lightest cat, Sidney has an extremely high metabolism. He eats all day and into the night, yet nary puts on a pound. Thus he is sometimes referred to as the elusive "Paper Clip." Quite the beggar, Sidney has an unmatched fondness for the contents of our plates, frequently seeking handouts from the breakfast, lunch, and dinner table. This distinct appreciation of food, combined with his ability to jump some six feet to lofty perches, have made for many an interesting tale spun about this black and white whiskered friend of Pine Brook Farm.

In a letter to me in college, dated January 21, 1992, my mother describes Sidney's fondness for all things delectable:

"I'm not sure where Sid is but I guess he's okay as long as I don't hear the clink of the glass cake cover against the cake dish in the kitchen. (Dad caught Sid licking the perimeter of the dish where icing had fallen.) That little oinker: Sid is a real chow-down kind of fella. I made crab dip for Vicki's Christmas party. Boy, you should have seen him and Abbey zoom in toward the can opener when I opened the crab. I gave them each a pinch in their dishes, guarding the remainder of the dip with my life. Now every time I head for the can opener Sid does his rendition of "Nobody Knows the Trouble I've Seen," in hopes that I'll feel sorry for him and hand over a morsel."

In another letter from February 24, 1992, Mom recounted this hysterical scene:

"Sunday morning, I had been having a bowl of cereal when there was a knock at the door (can you tell what's coming?...not what you think). When I returned to the kitchen, there was our little Sidney on the floor near your chair. You know my little white milk pitcher? Well, Sid was going around in circles trying to get it off his head!!! There was just about a quarter of an inch of milk in the bottom when I left the table. He obviously stuck his big head in, probably having a ball licking the milk off the insides as he inched his way to the bottom and that little bit of milk. (I hope it was worth it.) Lucky for him it came off just as I got near enough to do bodily harm, and Double Lucky for him that he didn't break my pitcher. After the shock wore off, I had to laugh."

Then there was the time when Sid grabbed an entire hamburger off our table but couldn't run away very fast because the patty weighed more than he did.

When Sid wasn't sporting ceramics or stealing seafood, there were plenty of other antics around the house. He enjoyed harassing my sister's dollhouse inhabitants by jumping onto the roof, leaning perilously over the edge, and smacking the people inside with his paws. And what cat can possibly avoid the temptation of the Christmas tree? We all know the trees are merely giant cat toys with no purpose other than for the pure amusement of our cats. On December 12, 1991, Mom wrote:

"This morning as I glanced into the sunroom, I saw a little white paw emerge from the inside branches of the Christmas tree and bat a small ornament to and fro. It was a weary site and gave new meaning to the term "live tree.""

In his advancing years, Sidney is best known for being patient, tolerant, and

quiet. He spends most of his days high atop the den bookshelf, peering down at my father with one eye open as Dad works on the computer. In the evenings he hops down into Dad's lap as the two sit together for a television program, stretched out comfortably in the old recliner. And yet he can still rough-and-tumble with the best of them, ever keeping a lookout for ways - no matter how small - to get into trouble as the years go by.

Sammie

The origins of the barn cat gang at Pine Brook Farm commenced with Sammie. Abandoned by the owner of an adjacent farm, my dad often spotted her at the edge of the woods during the construction of our house and barn. She was a beautiful orange tabby with subtle tan stripes, and even from a distance Dad could see a keen desire to trust in her eyes.

For many months, she refused to venture much farther from the cover of the woods despite Dad's efforts to connect with her. Every day he called to her and left food out, eventually sitting on the hillside and talking to her quietly. The "here, kitty kitty" approach was often used, and not just with Sammie, either. In fact, whenever a new cat is called, the current residents all look at each other as if to ask, "Who, me?"

Once he had walked a safe distance away, Sammie would cautiously make her way to the food dish, keeping an eye on him at all times. With each passing day he'd sit just a little closer as she ate, until he was right next to her. There were many more days of holding out his hand for her to sniff, until the magical moment when Sammie let him pet her.

She earned her name because it covered all the bases until Dad could verify her gender. Sammie spent her days roaming the woods and meadows of the farm, returning to the barn at night. Occasionally, she headed to the house for a snack or to say hello. This started a cheerful and comical routine for the barn cats. Each evening around 4:30, the group congregates outside the garage, awaiting the appearance of my father. Once he arrives, they follow him, single file, down the hill to the barn. It brings to mind the tale of the Pied Piper of Hamlin, but there's no questioning the motives behind their devout loyalty. Dinner is served in the heated and air conditioned tack room, which is filled with an old overstuffed armchair, cat beds, a window seat, snacks, a night light, and a radio. After many minutes of kind words and gentle pats, they are safely tucked in for the night. Were Santa to ask them what they wanted for Christmas, I doubt they could come up with even one thing.

The unspoken bond that formed between Sammie and Dad lasted for the rest of Sammie's lifetime, and illustrates two admirable qualities about my dad. One is that he has a special gift of communicating with animals in ways that not everyone understands. We sometimes call him Dr. Doolittle for his ability to "talk to the animals." And the second is that he never gives up. His personal mantra has always echoed that of Calvin Coolidge: "Press on… persistence and determination, alone, are omnipotent."

Midge

She may be small, but her bark is as bad as her bite. By far our most feisty and independent cat, Midge can certainly fend for herself among all the felines at Pine Brook Farm.

The heavens were shining upon her the day we brought Midge into our home. While jogging near the farm, my sister found this tiny kitten sitting helplessly in a gully by the side of a busy road. Barely eight weeks old, Midge was wet, dirty, and crying – a rather pathetic sight. I believe that her earliest experiences as a kitten must have toughened her against the harsh realities of a life outdoors.

Midgie rules the roost, or likes to think she does. No one can get away with petting her when she doesn't want to be touched. No one, that is, unless you don't mind a good scratch-and-hiss episode. You'll find her curled up, sleeping on the back of a wing chair. Carefully reach a hand out to stroke her fur. Ever on guard, she'll slowly open one eye and stare at you as if to mutter, Clint Eastwood style, "Go ahead, make my day." I have been adorned with many a battle scar from petting Midgie when I thought she wanted me to, when she was in fact luring me into her web of trickery just to appease her penchant for torment. And we won't even discuss attempts at bathing or claw trimming, both of which essentially require ground support from the National Guard.

Midge's throne consists of a worn wicker rocking chair in the kitchen that Mom and Dad refer to as "base." After a carefully calculated pounce or swat directed at one of the other house cats, Midge the Instigator regularly avoids full-scale brawls by making a hasty retreat for the arm of her chair. She all but declares "Safe! Ha ha, you can't touch me!" upon her arrival there, as Quincy and Sidney slink away, glowering over their shoulders. You get the distinct impression that they're off to plot their revenge. Not surprisingly, none of the other cats ever inhabit her chair.

Despite her thoroughly independent nature, Midge exhibits a nearly canine loyalty when it comes to "playing fetch." One of her favorite activities is retrieving – whether it be her cloth heart, rawhide string, or toy mouse. Throw it again and again, and she'll return to you carrying said item in her mouth. That is, until she decides to be lazy, play Devil's Advocate, and drop her cargo five feet away where you can't reach it. Regardless, you're still expected to get up, retrieve her toy, and give it another toss until she's had her fill. Midge routinely approaches Dad at dinner and taps his arm gently with her paw to get his attention, silently imploring him to play

fetch (or daring him not to, at which point the taps will become scratches).

Sure enough, Midge's demands for attention are quite insistent, and they only escalate when she isn't acknowledged. If Mom and Dad are sitting at the kitchen table eating or talking, and no one's paying Midgie any mind, she'll commence her tactic of prying open the lower cabinets with her paw as a purposeful distraction. Or she'll jump on the counter under the auspices of inspecting the leftovers. Her timing impeccable, she typically does this just when Mom is getting to the critical part of her story, or the punch line of a joke. This drives Mom nuts, but you'll almost always find Dad trying to contain his amusement at Midgie's antics – and failing miserably.

Midge has a mysterious fondness for the fax machine, madly dashing to it from across the house when she hears the familiar noises of its workings. She is fascinated by the paper edging out and curling from the machine, before falling to the floor.

I have been known, on occasion, to send her a personal fax from my office -- one that usually echoes our tenuous relationship.

"To: Midge
From: Jen
Date: December 14, 2003
RE: Santa is watching

Midge,
This fax is for you but pertains to all indoor felines of Pine Brook Farm.
-Get off the tree.
-Quit swatting the ornaments.
-Stop chewing on the Christmas potpourri.
-Keep your paws out of the floating candles.
-Ribbons are not for eating. Do you want to go to the V-E-T? I didn't think so.
-Stay off the counters – the eggnog is off limits.
You'd better behave yourselves or else Santa Cat will be filling your stockings with kitty litter.

Regards, JBF"

Despite her seemingly coarse exterior, Midge is not unaffectionate; it's simply a matter of cuddling on her terms. Every day she enjoys Mom's lap or footstool during reading and television time. She truly loves Mom best, though she twirls around and around her feet during the most inopportune moments - such as during the last critical minutes immediately before Thanksgiving Dinner is served. She maintains the "survival of the fittest" philosophy that she adopted long ago - and it shows - but Midgie is still a loving and treasured resident of the farm.

Marky

Another long-time barn inhabitant, Marky serves as our resident feline social director. He enjoys the company of all who visit and will be the first to "meet and greet," be they postman, farrier, or meter reader. Leave your car door open and you just might end up with a traveling companion for the trip home. I suspect the reason that no one has actually driven away with him yet is because he always opts for the driver's seat – and can therefore hardly be missed.

Marky was initially found simply hanging around the pine forest one frigid February night. After some careful grooming, copious amounts of good food, and much affection, he decided the farm was the place for him - and there's no part of it that he won't explore. If you're game for a walk, Mark loves to tag along. He'll accompany you on a short jaunt down to the creek, where you can sit on the wooden bridge and pet him. With legs dangling over the edge you can study the buzz of aquatic life below. He enjoys wandering through the underbrush of the woods on his daily expeditions. He'll follow you over hill and dale as you seek to share a bite of tart green apple or crunchy carrot with the horses.

I recall one summer morning when I was casually observing our equine friends near the water trough, after completing a few barn chores. Marky unabashedly walked right up to Spark, our very tall and intimidating - but friendly - horse, and sat in front of him. Spark's ears pricked forward in interest and he slowly lowered his giant head down to greet his little gray friend.

Marky stretched out his neck and they touched noses. Beneath their lowered eyelids I believe they asked each other, "And how are you today?" Friendship has no size restraints.

Marky is the proudest mouser on the farm. He leaves his "gifts" by the tack room door or sometimes in the garage, and sits nearby – patiently awaiting his praise. Despite his generous nature, I'm not sure he'd exactly be Santa's first choice for a helper. Interestingly, he never eats what he catches, and will often just play with his quarry before relinquishing it to the fields. His very best friend is our other barn cat, Simon, and you will usually spot the chubby pair together except when they go their separate ways to do their mousing.

One of Marky's favorite spots, particularly on hot summer days, is the mulch pile which largely sits in the shade of the dumpster. As the shade moves late in the afternoon, so does he. It is always amusing to drive around the corner as the barn comes into view and spot Marky, the Mulch King resting serenely atop his own personal "hill." I suspect he purposefully chose this place to observe the arrival of anyone visiting the farm so he could be the first to say "Welcome."

Simon

Whereas Marky is the "welcome wagon," Simon's sentiments are something more along the lines of "get lost." The most elusive of the Pine Brook Farm cats, Simon will usually head for the woods when anyone other than my father approaches. Somehow, all that running to hide has done nothing for his waistline which - like Santa's - can be politely described as "more than sufficient."

Like many of our cats, Simon "found us" rather than the other way around. My parents observed him perusing the farm one day, and soon thereafter learned that he actually belonged to one of our neighbors. His owners didn't particularly care whether he wandered away or not, which was quite opposite the reception he received at our farm. Simon wisely chose to stick around with us, and has enjoyed life as a barn cat ever since.

Aside from his girth, Simon looks quite the scholarly cat. His luxurious charcoal gray fur starkly contrasts his penetrating yellow eyes. I can easily picture him sitting upon a velvet tuffet next to a stack of dusty tomes, sporting round tortoiseshell spectacles and enjoying a saucer of cream. He appears

to be light years ahead of his cohorts in intelligence and sophistication, always choosing the loftiest and most cushioned of perches, even if it's the broad side his best friend, Marky.

While the outdoor cats are allowed to roam at will during the day, Dad brings them into the barn for the evening. They know the drill: Dad calls the cats to round them up, or they see him heading down the hill from the house and they follow. All, of course, except Simon. And so evenings are often spent looking for the wayward rogue. On occasion, we've found him hiding in the rafters behind some hay bales, probably quite amused by our wandering around, upstairs and down, calling his name. He's usually camouflaged in the bushes down by the creek, and chooses to venture forth nonchalantly only when he's good and ready. Yet this is not the end of his shenanigans. Refusing to cooperate, Simon dawdles as he waddles. He walks very slowly toward my dad and pauses many times to stop, look around, and maybe sit for a spell. He'll walk some more before deciding that cleaning his paw is an urgent matter, and before long he's bathed the rest of his rather large self. All too familiar with Simon's tardiness, Dad says it's usually just faster to go get him and carry him to the barn. I think we all know that

Simon enjoys calling the shots but moreover the special attention that results from his preference to be a "slow-poke."

When you are held in Simon's good graces, he is a most affectionate cat. All the barn felines enjoy their morning and evening attention from my dad. The problem is that he has only one lap. This is especially unfortunate for Simon who is less than agreeable when his turn is over. Dad's announcement, "It's time for you to get down now, Simon," is typically met with a growl. He'd be sure to run into problems when conveying his lengthy list of sophisticated Christmas wishes to Santa. But with Dad, as you might suspect, Simon gets a little more lap time than the other barn cats.

Quincy

Quincy's arrival at Pine Brook Farm was a special delivery of the most unusual kind. One summer morning, my father stood at the barn door pondering some chores that had to be done. His eyes swept over several pieces of equipment before he happened to glance off-handedly toward the driveway. Quite some distance away, there stood a gray cat who appeared to have a deeper level of understanding about things than most creatures. Her kitten waited tentatively by her side before the pair sat down and simply stared at my dad for several minutes. Finally, the mother cat began walking toward him, the kitten tagging alongside her. They stopped again, and the mom turned to her offspring in what appeared to be a gesture of reassurance.

She sat very still while the kitten trotted happily toward my father. The small gray and white feline was met with quiet words of comfort and gentle stroking of his soft fur. Despite Dad's attempts to coax the mom over as well, she looked at them one last time as if to relay her gratitude before turning to retreat down the driveway and into the woods.

To this day, my father believes that the mother cat

fully intended to leave her kitten on our farm with good reason. Could she not have somehow sensed that here was a safe place for the little one that would probably not survive on his own because of his trusting nature? Dad came to understand this about Quincy after a few days of observing his interactions with the current barn residents. So it was with both Quincy and the confident mother cat in mind, then, that Dad decided to make Quincy a housecat.

In much the same fashion that Marky and Simon expanded their middles (perhaps the genes for gray coat and chubbiness are linked), Quincy has availed himself of the ever-present philosophy at Pine Brook that no dish must be left empty. This has earned him titles such as McWaddle and Matoomba. When he's not whining pathetically for his more preferred types of high calorie food, he spends his days like most of the other house cats: curled up and snoozing in patches of

afternoon sunlight, observing the local wildlife, and serving as a purring lap warmer. Quincy sports an extra toe on each paw, a genetic condition known as polydactyly (you may have heard of this in Ernest Hemingway's cats). With his feet resembling oven mitts, he requires an even larger Christmas stocking, but there is more of him to love.

He's still as gentle and sweet as the day he first arrived at the farm with his mother. That is, with the exception of his two minor bad habits. For one thing, if you taunt him by putting any part of your limbs in front of his mouth, you will receive a nice nip. Not in the sense of a flesh wound, but rather he'll hold onto your skin with his sharp teeth and it doesn't exactly tickle. And for another, abandon your seat at the dinner table to retrieve a missing condiment and you'll immediately find him occupying it. Although my father couldn't possibly become irritated by the imposition, when Quincy looks up sweetly, Dad will still utter "Boy, you are rude," while pulling up another seat so as to avoid disturbing the greedy gray feline.

Sergio

Sergio might have been a gang member in a former life. Like Midge, he probably had a rough go at things starting out, as evidenced by his disposition under certain circumstances and his numerous scars. Our otherwise pristine white cat first appeared near the barn, venturing up to the loft on several occasions to rest during the day. Some days Dad joined him up there for a quiet chat. Then he'd be gone for a few days but would eventually return. My father again provided good food and kind words - Sergio was welcome to stay if that was his wish.

During one of these loft visits, Dad readily observed that Sergio had recently been in a horrible fight, most likely with a larger wild animal. My father had Sergio patched up and checked out, then returned home and decided to make him a house cat. Sergio's early adventures at the farm quickly revealed him to be extremely territorial. Dad would take him outside for exercise and play time, and soon learned to do this only after the barn cats were tucked in for the evening. Sergio took issue with the outdoor cats, chasing them away from the house if they so much as ventured nearby. While exploring the indoors, should

one of the barn cats appear at a window or glass door, Sergio would make it known to the outside cats that they had better get back to the barn or he was going to rearrange their color scheme. Sometimes he'd also get a little testy if another indoor cat ventured too close – but they could usually tell when he was about to turn into "Ivan the Terrible," as we liked to call him. On days like this, he was likely to top Santa's naughty list.

As it turned out, Sergio was quite content to inhabit the house during the day and the basement at night, where he had plenty of room away from Sidney, Midge, and Quincy. He enjoyed his evening walks with Dad and, later, his new best friend Lucy, during which they'd follow my father around in canine fashion. Quite the pair, Sergio in essence "adopted" Lucy as a little sister, strangely enough allowing her all manner of leniency as far as rough-housing went. She was permitted to

crawl and pounce on him, chase him up and down trees, and otherwise pester him to her heart's content. Pictured on the front cover of this book, they were also involved in "helping" to decorate for Christmas by meowing out orders from atop their ladder perches.

His docile, loving side was also revealed by how he slept on my dad's desk and literally chirped his contentment when petted while being held upside down. Sergio will always hold a special place in my father's heart. He passed away after only a few short years with us and we will forever recall the laughter and happiness he brought, and how he looked after Lucy with such purity and joy of spirit.

Lucy

H e probably wouldn't admit to this, but I think Lucy might be Dad's favorite among all the felines of Pine Brook Farm. This might have something to do with the fact that he most likely saved her life.

It was the Friday morning before the Fourth of July, and already the heaviness of the air indicated that another sticky, sweltering day was ahead. Dad had driven sixteen miles to a nearby town to retrieve his chain saw from the area repair shop. In the parking lot, he spotted a small calico cat in dire need of medical care. Her coat was filthy, her eyes and nose exuding thick mucous, and her tail was far shorter than it should have been. She walked right over to my dad for some attention and then headed for the slight relief of a shade tree.

In the shop, Dad inquired of the woman behind the counter, "What's with the short-tailed cat outside?" She informed him that the employees feed a number of stray cats regularly seen around the store. Outside, Dad once again mulled over what to do but answers weren't forthcoming. While my father's philosophy toward adopting stray cats has always been, "If they come, I will care for them," Mom understandably has her limits. After all, they already had eight cats to care for. And besides, this wasn't exactly his cat to rescue. Dad packed up the chain saw and headed home.

Naturally, he thought about the little calico all weekend, but never mentioned a word to my mother about it. Monday the Fourth rolled around and he was out running errands. While picking up a few supplies for the barn, Dad decided to revisit the repair shop just to see if the cat was still there. Sure enough, she was lying miserably under the same tree, tail twitching back and forth as if it echoed her restlessness. He opened the door of his truck, called her over, and she lethargically walked toward him. He put her on the seat and headed home, doubtful that she would survive. The version that Mom heard involved a "very sick cat found by the side of the road."

Because of the congestion associated with her illness, Lucy usually had difficulty breathing and uttered sounds that resembled the quacking of a duck. Thus she soon earned the nickname of "Ducky." She spent her recuperation in a special basement room that had been converted to house feline guests of the farm. After extensive treatment, "Little Lucy" healed quite well, broken tail and all.

Our very fortunate cat enjoyed many a day exploring the house and yard with her surrogate older brother and best friend, Sergio. Since Sergio's passing, Porky has assumed the role of new companion and playmate to Lucy. Although quite aged, she still acts very much like a kitten – seizing each day of the life she could have easily lost. Lucy brings out the child in all of us, and serves as a gentle reminder that our time on this planet should never be taken for granted.

Incidentally, it took my mother about two days to discover Dad's little fib about how he crossed paths with Lucy. After forty years, she knows when he's fudging the truth. He confessed and told her the real story behind the catnapping.

Porky

Porky, the great big cat with the little porcine nose, demonstrates once again what can happen with a little time and patience. For about a year, my father observed a black and white cat near the entrance to our driveway. He inhabited a rocky culvert there that ran under the main road. Every time the two would meet, Dad would make himself comfortable on the embankment and start up a conversation.

After many months, he noticed the cat exploring near the barn, and ultimately the house. Dad sat for many hours, calling the cat, offering food, and sometimes simply watching him. Porky finally approached my father, tentatively sniffing his hand, and the connection was made. Now you would see him everywhere during the day – sleeping in the window boxes, lounging in the garage, and peering into the house through the French doors. Yet when night fell, he always returned to the culvert.

Fortunately, Porky eventually conceded and allowed himself to become an official barn cat. This meant exploring the grounds during the day and being tucked in with the others at night. He enjoyed companionship, a soft place to sleep, and plenty of

food. However, Porky turned out to be somewhat of a bully toward the other barn cats. Dad thought he liked to show off, and just wanted to play but didn't quite understand how since he'd spent so much time as a feral cat.

Dad brought Porky up to the house where he became an official inhabitant of the garage and basement. There he took long walks in the evening with

my father and Lucy, with whom he became great chums. When it was time to come in for the evening meal, Porky could always coax my dad into a game of "let's run around the bush and see if you can catch me." Porky sometimes waited for Dad to return to the house after finishing the barn chores. As Dad started walking up the hill, Porky would run down to meet him. After being picked up for a hug and put back down again, he liked to run past Dad and swat him on the pants leg. It was as if Porky was saying, "Tag, you're it."

Porky was another of our many "lap cats," particularly on spring and summer evenings when Mom and Dad would relax in their comfortable lawn chairs, gazing out over the pastures while the horses grazed in the setting sun. Dad says Porky

most enjoyed being held. Pork would purr louder than a motorcycle, tucking his head under my father's chin - a comfort like no other. They shared daily rituals that my Dad never tired of, and neither did Porky. Like all of our cats, he reminded us to "give and ye shall receive."

Amanda

The newest member of the Pine Brook Farm cat clan, Amanda registered on my dad's stray cat radar the day he heard her whining and crying as she strolled along the edge of the woods near the barn. Minutes later, after quickly sensing that Dad was trustworthy, she was carried to the tack room and made comfortable.

One might wonder if every and any cat that steps one paw onto the farm becomes a permanent resident. While that has largely been the case, I must point out that with all animals found roaming the property - whether cats, dogs, or even horses - my parents always make a diligent effort to locate the owners. They prepare and hang up signs, place newspaper advertisements, and call local animal shelters to inquire about lost pets. Over the many years they have been fortunate to reunite many of the lost dogs with their owners, but very few of the cats. Amanda is another example of this.

After a few days of being sequestered from the other barn cats, Amanda was introduced to her new roommates, Marky and Simon. While they got along splendidly outside the barn, she'd grown so fond of her posh accommodations that she'd defensively chase them out of the tack room if they tried to enter what had, only days earlier, been *their* residence. Like a toddler, Amanda had to be taught to share.

Amanda is the first barn cat to greet my father in the morning. She walks to the edge of the long green bench in the tack room and stands on her hind legs so he can pet her. She likes to help with the barn chores, following Dad outside to feed the horses their morning hay. And in the evening, unlike Simon the Straggler, she's the first to head to the barn for dinner, trotting out from the woods the second she's called.

Cats provide us with the gift of fun every day. One of her favorite things to do is crouch down in the small drainage ditch near the barn and play hide-and-seek with Marky and Simon. Sometimes Dad joins this amusing game, as they all race around together before returning to the chores of the day. Amanda reminds us to "stop and enjoy the view," while we remain thankful that this beautiful black cat ever decided to wander over to our neck of the woods.

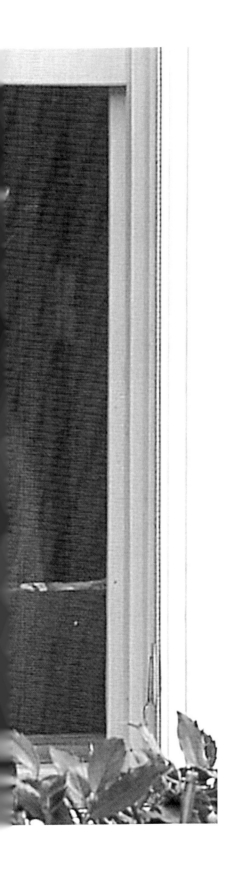

To Be Continued...

While most of our cats were friendly from the start, some needed extra care and attention before they could learn to trust humans again. We'll never know what their life was like prior, or what experiences they had. But now they're our companions for life, as we share in their humor, affection, and love. And so the spirit of giving lives on.

This story is to be continued by you - the reader. For those of you who are already familiar with the joy our feline friends can bring us, may you spread the word about the pleasures of having a cat in one's life. And for our readers who have yet to experience such a warm and rewarding relationship with a cat, we hope that you'll consider providing the gift of a loving home for one. The moment a cat jumps up on your lap and gazes deeply into your eyes, you will remember how very much you've both been blessed. I think Santa's doing that very thing right now.

Adopt a Cat

Paws down, cats make terrific pets. Some 33 percent of households in this country (38.2 million) have at least one cat, and of those, 56 percent own more than one. But there just aren't homes for them all.

According to the Humane Society of the United States (HSUS), between six and eight million dogs and cats enter shelters annually, and only about half are adopted. That means between 3,000,000 and 4,000,000 are euthanized every year.

From early spring to autumn, the kitten season leaves thousands – many of them orphans – to fend for themselves in cities, suburbs, and in the country. Stray cats face an onslaught of threats that they only perpetuate when they, in turn, breed: starvation, severe weather, injuries from wildlife and motor vehicles, and abuse. Meanwhile, shelters are forced to contend with serious overcrowding at times and must unfortunately base their decisions on available space, and not just on the health and personality of cats. Overcrowding stresses the cats and staff alike. Many shelter employees and volunteers take cats home temporarily to prevent euthanasia. These individuals are often already spread thin in terms of the time and money they have available to use on their own pets.

Animal shelters are the best place to adopt a new pet. When you adopt from a shelter instead of buying from a commercial source, you are helping to reduce the number of unwanted strays in your area. These safe havens are usually nonprofit organizations and therefore rely on private donations. Most charge an adoption fee to partially supplement the costs of feeding, vaccinating, and medicating their residents. This cost is substantially less than what you'd pay a pet store or breeder. Many shelters provide follow-up assistance with behavioral training or veterinary care, and nearly all will refer you to providers of these services. To find your local shelter, check online or look in your phone book under "animal shelter" or "humane society."

PetSmart is an excellent place to adopt a cat. Since its establishment in 1987, the company has chosen not to sell dogs and cats, but rather to assist animal welfare organizations by encouraging pet adoptions. As of August 11, 2011, the company has placed 4,594,267 animals in private homes.

One such welfare group is Animal Rescue, Inc., which operates a cattery near Putty Hill, Maryland, as well as a 33-acre farm in Pennsylvania. Animal Rescue was founded in 1976 by Grace Froelich, a woman who faced eviction if she did not give up her cat. Grace kept her cat, bought a new home, and after she settled in, the strays began showing up. She would feed these dogs and cats and let them stay, adamant that they would never be homeless again. Eventually, Grace moved toward adopting out those that she could, beginning a more than thirty-year mission of finding loving families for stray animals. She coined the phrase "forever home" to reflect that, while she hoped every stray would be adopted, if they never found a home, they would always be welcome as part of the Animal Rescue family.

Today, with the assistance of many dedicated volunteers, Animal Rescue cares for approximately one hundred dogs and several hundred cats at a time, most of whom are available for adoption. The organization sponsors low-cost spay and neuter programs and operates a Crisis Intervention Program to provide assistance to elderly, ill, and infirm pet owners.

New animals enter shelters like these daily, so if your local facility doesn't have the type of cat you're after, wait a few days and check back, or have your name

placed on a waiting list. There are always plenty of kittens, and approximately thirty percent of animals entering shelters are pure-bred -- if these are things you're considering. In addition, many shelters maintain web sites linked to online databases that list cats available for adoption. Simply enter your zip code and preferences and you'll see an inventory, usually accompanied by photographs and personality traits, that may help you narrow your search.

Animal shelters provide an added benefit: employees carefully evaluate the health, disposition, and behavior of their resident cats. Consider adopting an older cat; they are so eager for a new home and they're harder to place with new families. Shelter workers rely on their notes about a cat's temperament to create the perfect match between feline and family, based on the ages of any other pets or children.

The problem of overpopulation can be further reduced if every cat owner spays or neuters their pet. The average fertile female cat produces three litters per year of four to six kittens each. After seven years, that mom and her offspring can yield 420,000 kittens. Even if your cat gets out one time, she or he can mate. Fixing your cat reduces this hormonally-induced desire to roam, and makes them a bit more laid back and easier to train. They won't keep you up at night with their incessant howling and scratching at the window. Altered cats also live longer. Your female cat will have a reduced risk of breast cancer, and zero threat of uterine or ovarian cancer. Your male will avoid testicular and prostate cancers and face less of a threat of medical conditions such as hernia. Despite the popular myth that your cat will become overweight and lazy, this is not the case – too many calories and lack of exercise are to blame, not spaying or neutering. And even if you think you'll find homes for all the kittens, there go six homes that could have been used for current shelter inhabitants.

In addition to fixing your cat, you can also do your part to help any of the 4,000 to 6,000 U.S. animal shelters in a number of ways. Consider volunteering your time. You might spend your afternoon grooming, feeding, or just hanging out and playing with the cats and kittens. Shelters can always use your monetary donations or household items like food, toys, old towels and blankets, and other supplies. Many shelters maintain "wish lists" of much needed items, especially during the holidays.

Lastly, spread the word. Support legislation that helps animals and urge your local officials to do the same. Report issues such as injuries, strays, cruelty, and neglect. And encourage everyone you know to provide a loving home for this most wonderfully clever, faithful, and just plain fun animal: The Cat.

The following animal advocacy organizations provide stray animal databases and additional information about pet care and adoption. A portion of the proceeds from this book will be donated to Animal Rescue, in support of their adoption program and resident care.

Animal Rescue, Inc.
2 Heritage Farm Drive
New Freedom, PA 17349
(717) 993-9645
www.animalrescueinc.org

Mailing Address:
Animal Rescue, Inc.
P.O. Box 35
Maryland Line, MD 21105

Adopt-a-Pet.com
P.O. Box 7
Redondo Beach, CA 90277
(800) 728-3273
www.adoptapet.com

American Society for the
Prevention of Cruelty to Animals
424 E. 92nd St.
New York, NY 10128-6804
(212) 876-7700
www.aspca.org

American Pet Association
(800) 272-7387
www.apapets.com

Animal Planet's Petfinder
www.petfinder.com

The Fund for Animals
P.O. Box 367
Murchison, TX 75778
(903) 469-3811
www.fundforanimals.org

Humane Society of the United States
2100 L St., NW
Washington, D.C. 20037
(202) 452-1100
www.humanesociety.org

PETS911
16413 N. 91st Street, Suite C100
Scottsdale, AZ 85260
(480) 889-2640
www.pets911.com

PetSmart, Inc.
19601 North 27th Ave.
Phoenix, AZ 85027
(800) 738-1385
www.petsmart.com

World Animal Net – USA
19 Chestnut Square
Boston, MA 02130
(617) 524-3670
www.worldanimal.net

About the Author

Jennifer Foulk teaches undergraduate biology and works part-time as a freelance writer and graphic artist. A conservation biologist by training, she is very active in working to protect the environment. She enjoys reading, running, the great outdoors, and spending time with her husband, children, and three glorious cats.

About the Photographer

Robert Biser is the founder and president of PermaWell, Inc., a horse farm consulting business and world-wide distributor of UltraGuard™ vinyl horse fencing. An amateur photographer for more than forty years, his favorite subjects have always been pets and wildlife. Robert takes time to enjoy the view at Pine Brook Farm, his home in Maryland, with his wife, Kim, their three horses, and ten funny felines. He also provides a foster home for as many as ten homeless cats at a time, through Animal Rescue, Inc. of Maryland and the PetSmart Adoption Program.

CPSIA information can be obtained
at www.ICGtesting.com
Printed in the USA
LVIW021913171212

312072LV00011B